THE FIRST BOOK OF MEZZO-SOPRANO/ALTO SOLOS

compiled by Joan Frey Boytim

ISBN 978-0-7935-0365-0

G. SCHIRMER, Inc.

DISTRIBUTED BY

HAL•LEONARD®
CORPORATION

7777 W. BLUEMOUND RD. P.O. BOX 13819 MILWAUKEE, WI 53213

PREFACE

Repertoire for the beginning voice student, whether teenager, college student, or adult, always poses a great challenge for the voice teacher because of the varied abilities and backgrounds the students bring to the studio. This series of books for soprano, mezzo-soprano and alto, tenor, and baritone and bass provides a comprehensive collection of songs suitable for first and second year students of any age, but is compiled with the needs of the young singer in mind.

In general, students' first experiences with songs are crucial to their further development and continued interest. Young people like to sing melodious songs with texts they can easily understand and with accompaniments that support the melodic line. As the student gains more confidence, the melodies, the texts, and the accompaniments can be more challenging. I have found that beginning students have more success with songs that are short. This enables them to overcome the problems of musical accuracy, diction, tone quality, proper technique, and interpretation without being overwhelmed by the length of the song.

Each book in this series includes English and American songs, spirituals, sacred songs, and an introduction to songs in Italian, German, French and Spanish. Many students study Spanish in the schools today, and most studio volumes do not include songs in this language; therefore, we have included two for each voice type.

Several songs in the collections have been out of print in recent years, while others have been previously available only in sheet form. Special care has been taken to avoid duplication of a great deal of general material that appears in other frequently used collections. These new volumes, with over thirty songs in each book, are intended to be another viable choice of vocal repertoire at a very affordable price for the teacher and student.

Each book contains several very easy beginning songs, with the majority of the material rated easy to moderately difficult. A few songs are quite challenging musically, but not strenuous vocally, to appeal to the student who progresses very rapidly and who comes to the studio with a great deal of musical background.

In general, the songs are short to medium in length. The ranges are very moderate, yet will extend occasionally to the top and the bottom of the typical voice. The majority of the accompaniments are not difficult, and are in keys that should not pose major problems. The variety of texts represented offers many choices for different levels of individual student interest and maturity.

In closing, I wish to thank Richard Walters at Hal Leonard Publishing for allowing me to be part of this effort to create this new series of vocal collections. We hope that these books will fill a need for teachers and students with suitable, attractive and exciting music.

Joan Frey Boytim

CONTENTS

AMERICAN LULLABY

words and music by
Gladys Rich

Grazioso

mf *legatissimo*

Hush-a - bye, you sweet lit-tle ba - by, And don't you cry_ an-y

more; Dad-dy is down at his stock-brok-er's of-fice A -

ba - by like you.

Hush - a - bye, you sweet lit - tle ba - by, And

close those pret - ty blue eyes. Moth-er has gone to her

week-ly bridge par - ty To get her wee ba - by the prize.

Nurs-ie will turn the ra-di-o on,__

So you can hear__ a sleep-y-time song,__

Sung by a la-dy whose poor heart must long__ For a

ba-by like you!__

_mf_ _mp a tempo_

rall.

dim. e rall.

L'ANNEAU D'ARGENT
(The Silver Ring)

Cécile Chaminade

Andante. (♩ = 104.)
very gently and tranquilly, but not dragging. **p**

pp *With a scarcely perceptible arpeggio.*

2 Ped.

The sil-ver ring so
Le cher an-neau d'ar-

dear that once thou gav-est me, Fast in its ti-ny
gent que vous m'a-vez don-né, Garde en son cercle é-

cir- -clet our vows yet en - clos - es; The
troit_____ nos pro - mes - ses en - clo - ses; De

10

flow-ers en-twines, tho' fad-ed they may be; So this poor sil-ver
cor le bou-quet a-lors qu'il est fa-né, Tel 'l'humble an-neau d'ar-

ring, that once thou gav-est me, Fast in its ti-ny
gent que vous m'a-vez don-né Garde en son cer-cle é-

cir-clet our vows yet en-clos-es. So, when for-get-ting
troit nos pro-mes-ses en-clo-ses. Aus-si, lors-que vien-

all, my heart at length re-pos-es, In the last
dra l'ou-bli de tou-tes cho-ses, Dans le cer-

DIE BEKEHRTE
(The Converted One)

Johann Wolfgang von Goethe

Max Stange

Andantino.

Bei dem Glanz der A - bend - rö - the ging ich still den
As I roam'd the woods at lei - sure In the eve - ning

Wald ent - lang,
hour so still,

Da - mon sass und
Da - mon sat and

blies die Flö - te, dass es von den Fel - sen klang:
piped for plea - sure, E - cho an - swer'd from the hill:

so la re
so la re

Und_ ich sag-te, bla - se wie - der, und der gu - te Jun - ge blies: so
But_ I bade him still_ be play - ing, And the kind - ly youth complied: so

la_____ re la_____ la
la_____ re la_____ la

la_____ la la.
la_____ la la.

Mei - ne Ruh' ist nun_ ver - lo - ren, mei - ne
Now, a - las, I wan - der lone - ly, All_ my

Freu - de floh da - von, und __ ich hör' vor mei - nen
joy is turn'd to pain; Dream - ing, wak - ing, hear __ I

Oh - ren im - mer nur den al - ten Ton:
on - ly Da - mon's sweet and ten - der strain:

so la_____ re la_____
so la_____ re la_____

__ la la_____ la la.
__ la la_____ la la.

DER BLUMENSTRAUSS
(The Nosegay)

Felix Mendelssohn

Sie wan-delt im Blu-men-gar - -ten und mu-stert den bun - ten Flor,_____ und al-le die Klei - nen war - -ten und schau-en zu ihr em-por. „Und seid ihr denn Früh-lings-bo - -ten, ver -

She strays in the flow-er-gar - -den, Sur-vey-ing the gau - dy scene,_____ While all the wee flow-ers are wait - -ing, And gaz-ing on her, their queen. "And are ye the her-alds of Spring - -tide, Fore -

So ü - ber-schaut sie die
Light - ly the flow - ers en -

Ha - - be und ord - net den lieb - li - chen Strauss, ____ und
twin - - ing, How deft - ly her fin - gers toil: ____ She

reicht dem Freunde die Ga - - be, und weicht sei - nem Bli - cke aus. Was
hands them to one ___ who nears her, A - void - ing his gaze the while. What

Blu - men und Far - ben mei - nen, o deu - tet, o fragt das
flow - ers and hues be - to - ken, Di - vine it, oh, ask ___ it

19

THE CHERRY TREE

Margaret Rose

Armstrong Gibbs

Time of performance 2 –2¼ mins.

The sad, sweet birds of the Spring-

time are sing - ing a - gain to me._____

_ They sing of the fro - zen riv - ers,_____

Pi - ping soft and low _____ Till I

think I hear _____ your foot - steps danc - ing

poco rit. *a tempo*

a - cross the snow.

Sing of my love in the North - land _____ As my love once

sang to me. _____

Hush, birds! the cher-ry in si - lence Is

let - ting her pet - als fall ⸺⸺⸺⸺ For

one whose danc - ing foot - steps Will nev - er

perdendosi

come ⸺⸺⸺ at all. ⸺⸺⸺⸺⸺

CHI VUOL LA ZINGARELLA

Giovanni Paisiello

Chi vuol la zin-ga-rel-la gra- ziosa ac-corta e bel-la? Si- guori, ec-co-la qua, si-gnori, ec-co-la qua. Le don-ne sul bal-co- ne

Who'll try the Gip-sy pretty, So winning, wise and wit-ty, As one and all may see, As one and all may see? For la-dies at their win- dow

27

qua, si - gnori, ec - co - la__ qua. Le don-ne sul bal -
me, come one and all__ to__ me. For ladies at their

co - ne so bene in-do-vi - nar. I giovani al can-
win - dow Their fortune I can tell, The laddies at the

to - ne so meglio stuzzi - car. A vecchi in-na-mo -
inn, too, I can amuse as well. When old men feel love

ra - ti, a vecchi in-na-mo-ra - ti scal-dar fo__ le cer-vel-la. Chi
burn-ing I set their heads a - turn-ing, I__ set their heads a - turning. Who'll

col canto

CLOUD-SHADOWS

Katharine Pyle

James H. Rogers

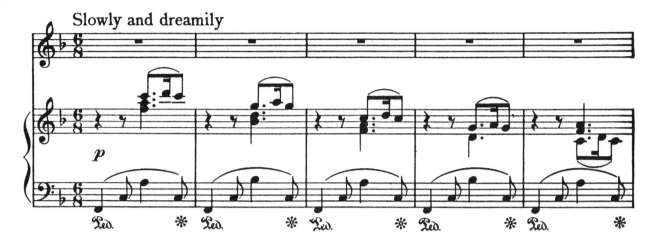

I wish I could ride on the shad-ows of clouds That drift a-cross the

hill; O-ver the mead-ow and out of sight They sweep so smooth and still.

O - ver the dai - sy field they passed, And not a dai - sy stirr'd; They

moved like char - i - ots grand and slow, But nev - er a sound was heard.

wish I could ride on the shad-ows of clouds, Could ride till, the jour-ney done, I'd

find my-self at the end of the world, Where the earth and the sky are one.

CHRISTOPHER ROBIN IS SAYING HIS PRAYERS
(Vespers)

A. A. Milne

H. Fraser-Simson

Slower again

cold's so cold, And the hot's so hot. Oh! God bless Dad - dy I

Quickening

quite for - got. If I o - pen my fin - gers a lit - tle bit more, I can

see Nan-ny's dress-ing gown on the door. It's a beau - ti - ful blue, but it

Slower

has - n't a hood. Oh! God bless Nan - ny and make her good.

36

Again quickening

Mine has a hood and I lie in bed And pull the hood right

o - ver my head. And I shut my eyes and I curl up small, And

A little slower

no-bod - y knows that I'm there at all. Oh! Thank you God, for a love - ly day, And

Quickening

what was the oth - er I had to say? I said "Bless Dad - dy" so

CRABBED AGE AND YOUTH

William Shakespeare

Maude Valérie White

CRUCIFIXION

African American spiritual
arranged by John Payne

bowed His head an' died, An' He nev-er said a mum-bal-lin'

word, He bowed His head an' died, An' He nev-er said a mum-bal-lin'

word, Not a word, not a word, not a word.

EVENSONG

Constance Morgan

Liza Lehmann

- ly now sings.

A - cross the lawn lie

sha - dows. So still, so deep,

Dear, lov - ing An - gels, pass not by, Hush me to

sleep.

EL MAJO TIMIDO
(The Timid Majo)

Llega a mi reja y me mira por la noche un majo.
Que en cuanto me ve y suspira se va calle abajo.
¡Ah! Que tío mas tardío,
Si asi se pasa la vida,
Estoy divertida.

At night, under my window, a majo* comes to look at me.
After he sees me, he sighs and goes on his way.
Ah! What a dull man.
If this is how it's going to be,
Some fun I'll have!

* majo is an untranslatable word for a dashing, handsome
lover

Enrique Granados

pi - ra se vá ca - lle a - ba - jo

¡Ay que ti - o mas tar - di - o

Sia- si se pa- sa la vi - da es - toy di - ver - ti - da

GO 'WAY FROM MY WINDOW

words and music by
John Jacob Niles

both-er me no__ more._____ I'll
long as song - birds sing._____ I'll
on ac-count of__ you._____ Go
real-ly did love best._____ Go 'way from my win-dow, Go

'way__ from my door, Go 'way, 'way, 'way from my bed-side And

rit. e dim.

both-er me no more,__ And both-er me no__ more.

ICI-BAS!
(Here Below)

Sully Prudhomme

Gabriel Fauré

To be sung in parlando style

I - ci - bas les lè - vres ef - fleu - rent Sans
Here be - low, where lips_light-ly sev - er And

rien lais-ser de leur ve - lours,
leave no trace of beau - ty's reign,

Je rêve___ aux bai-
I dream_ of kiss- es

sers qui de-meu - rent Tou - jours!_____
fond that for-ev - er Re - main._____

THE LAMB

William Blake

Theodore Chanler

JESUS WALKED THIS LONESOME VALLEY

arranged by Gordon Myers

Andante

1. Je - sus walked____ this lone-some val - ley, He had to

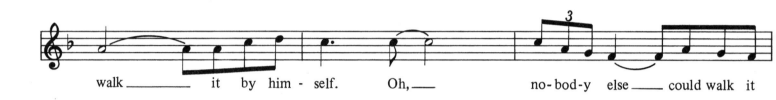

walk____ it by him - self. Oh,____ no-bod-y else____ could walk it

for him, He had to walk it by____ him - self. 2. We must

walk____ this lone-some val - ley, we have to walk____ it by our-

p

selves. Oh, _____ no-bod-y else _____ can walk it

for us, we have to walk it by _____ our-

selves. 3. We must clasp _____ our hands to-

geth-er, we have to clasp _____ them in the air. Oh, __

for us, the prayer of broth - er - hood— is there. 5. Je - sus

walked———— this lone-some val-ley, He had to walk———— it by him -

self. Oh,— no-bod-y else——— could walk it for him, He had to

walk it by— him - self.—————

Note: To dramatize 'loneliness', the last two measures
of the accompaniment may be omitted.

THE LASS FROM THE LOW COUNTREE

John Jacob Niles

Andante espressivo

Oh, he was a lord of high de-gree, And she was a lass from the Low Coun-tree, But she loved his lord-ship so ten-der-ly! Oh, sor - row, sing

sor - row! Now she sleeps in the val - ley where the wild - flow - ers nod, And

no one knows she loved him but her - self and God.___ One

morn, when the sun was on the mead, He passed by her door on a

milk-white steed;__ She smil-ed and she spoke, but he paid no heed. Oh,

sor - row, sing sor - row! Now she sleeps in the val - ley where the

wild - flow-ers nod, And no one knows she loved him but her - self and God.__

If you be a lass from the Low Coun-tree, Don't

THE LORD IS MY SHEPHERD

Peter Tchaikovsky
adapted and arranged by
Richard Maxwell and
Fred Feibel

Psalm 23

Andante con licenza

The Lord is my shep - herd; I shall not want.____ He mak - eth me to lie down in green

Tempo I⁰

Sure - ly good - ness and mer - cy shall fol - low me all the

days of my life: and I will dwell in the house of the

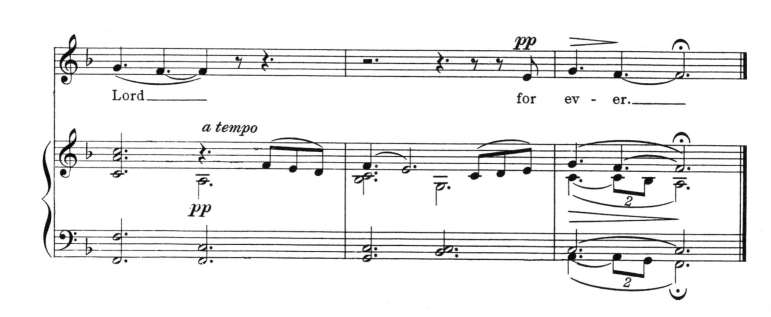

Lord for ev - er.

SILENT NOON

Dante Gabriel Rossetti

Ralph Vaughan Williams

peace.　　The pas-ture　gleams and glooms 'Neath bil - low-ing

skies　that　scat-ter　and a - mass.

Poco più mosso

All　round　our　nest,　far　as　the　eye　can　pass,　Are

74

LOVELIEST OF TREES

A.E. Housman*

John Duke

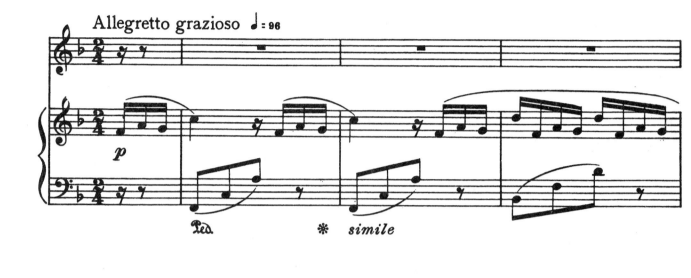

*Poem from "A Shropshire Lad." Printed by permission of Grant Richards, London, publisher.

MORNING

from the "Atlanta Constitution"
by Frank L. Stanton

Oley Speaks

*From the "Atlanta Constitution;" used by permission.

Copyright, 1931, by G. Schirmer, Inc.

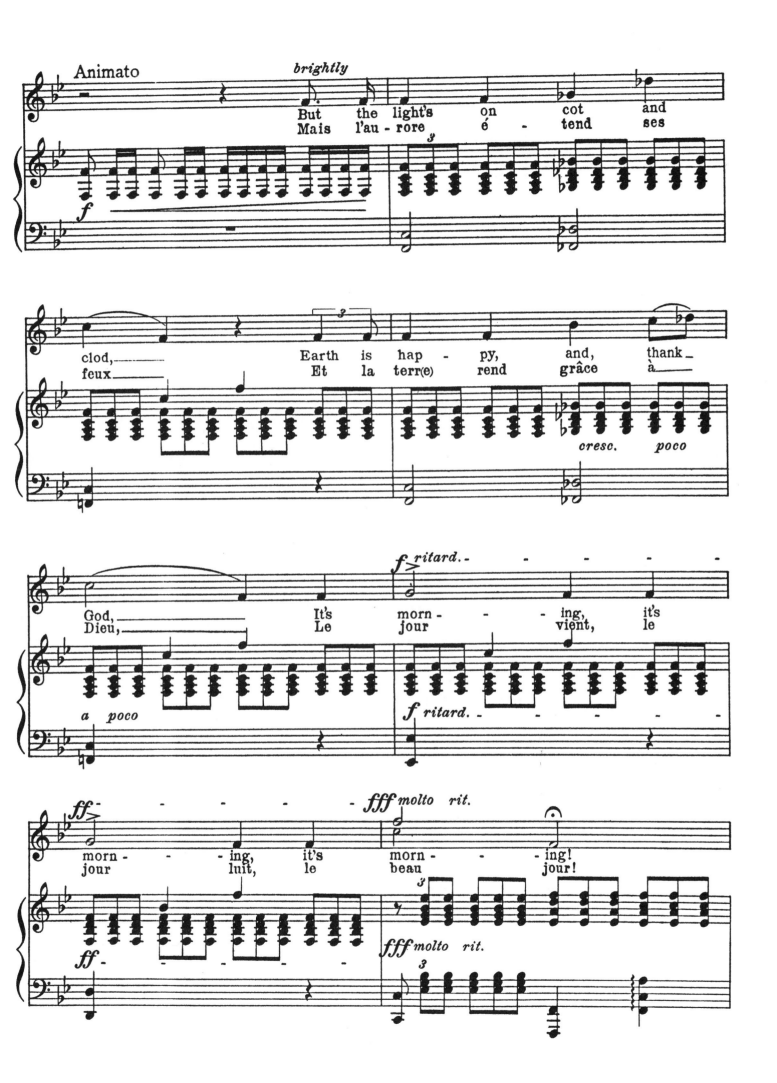

PRAYER

Hermann Hagedorn

David W. Guion

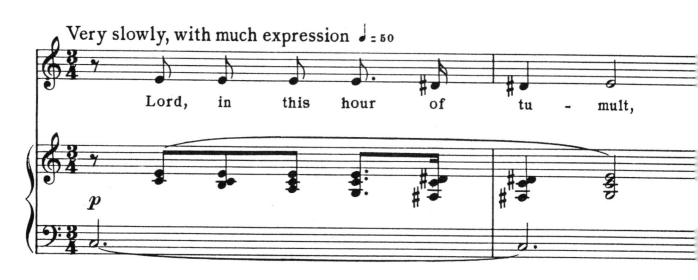

Lord, in this hour of tu - mult,

Lord, in this night of fears,___ Keep o - pen, oh, keep

o - pen My eyes, my heart, my ears.

PREGÚNTALE A LAS ESTRELLAS

Latin American folksong
arranged by Edward Kilenyi

-gún-tale á to-do el mun - do si no es pro-fun-do mi pa - de - cer.
ask of all cre - a - tion If thou art not, love, my soul's one cry.

colla voce

Ya nun-ca du - des que yo te quie - ro, Que por tí
Ah! doubt not dear - est, that I a - dore thee, For thee I

mf

colla voce

mue - ro, lo - co de a-mor; A na-die a - mas, á na-die
per - ish dis-traught with love; Thou lov-est no one, Thy heart beats

colla voce P cresc.

quie - res, O - ye las que-jas, o - ye las que-jas de mi a - mor.___
cold - ly, Oh! hear the plead-ing, Oh! hear the plead-ing of my fond love.___

f

Pre -
Go

-gún-ta-le á las flo-res, si mis a-mo-res les cuen-to yo, Cuan-
ask of the sweet flowers bloom-ing *If of my sor-rows I told not all.* *Go*

-do la ca-lla-da no-che cie-rra su bro-che, su-spi-ro yo, Pre-
ask of the wild birds sing-ing *If I sigh when the night doth fall.* *Go*

-gún-ta-le á las a-ves, si tu no sa-bes lo que es a-mor, Pre-
ask of the dew-y mea-dows *If thy love holds not my heart in thrall.* *Go*

-gún-tale á to-do el pra-do, si no he lu-cha-do con mi do - lor.
ask of all cre - a - tion If for thee, dar-ling, I pine, and call.

Tú bien com - pren - des, que yo te quie - ro, Que por tí
Ah! hear me dear - est, how well I love thee, For thee I

mue - ro, so - lo por tí; Por-que te quie-'ro, bien de mi
per - ish dis-traught with love. My on-ly so - lace is to a-

vi - da, So -lo en el mun-do, so-lo en el mun-do, te quie-ro á ti.
-dore thee. My heart's de - vo-tion, my heart's de - vo-tion I of-fer thee.

O REST IN THE LORD

from *Elijah*

Psalm 37

Felix Mendelssohn

OH SLEEP, WHY DOST THOU LEAVE ME?

from *Semele*

William Congreve

George Frideric Handel

*The Editor's piano accompaniment is founded on Handel's unfigured bass.

OPEN OUR EYES

Frederic West MacDonald

Will C. Macfarlane

104

DER SCHWUR
(The Vow)

Erik Meyer-Helmund

One day he saw his sweet - heart Be-
Als Tags da-rauf er wie - -der den

neath the eld - er fair, And watch'd her ty _ ing ap - - ples Up
Weg zur Trauten fand, sass Gret-chen auf dem Flie - -der, da-

on the branches there!
ran sie Ae-pfel band.

THE SKY ABOVE THE ROOF

Mabel Dearmer
based on Verlaine

Ralph Vaughan Williams

The sky a-bove the roof Is calm and sweet: A tree a-bove the roof Bends

in the heat.	A bell from out the blue Drow-si-ly rings: A bird from out the blue Plain - - - tive-ly sings.

Ah God! a life is here, Sim-ple and fair,

Mur-murs of strife are here Lost _____ in the _____ air.

Why dost thou weep, O

heart, Poured out in tears? What hast thou

done, O heart,........... With thy spent years?

f *colla voce* *pp*

Più lento.

THE STATUE AT CZARSKOE-SELO

Alexander Pushkin*

Cesar Cui

*English words based on the version by Charles Fonteyn Manney, Copyright, 1929, by Oliver Ditson Company.

Copyright, 1946, by G. Schirmer, Inc.

VOLKSLIEDCHEN
(In The Garden)

Franz Ruckert

Robert Schumann

WIE MELODIEN
(A Thought Like Music)

Klaus Groth   Johannes Brahms

A thought, like mu - sic, _ hold - ing My
Wie Me - lo - di - en _ zieht es mir

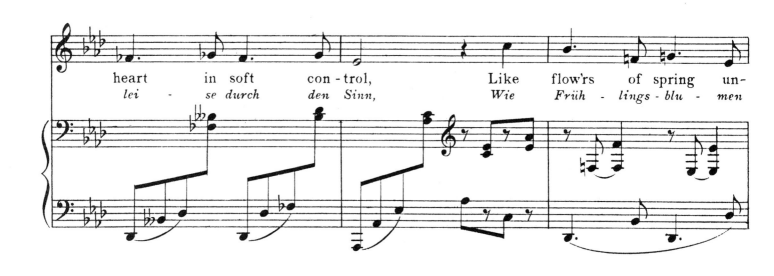

heart in soft con - trol, Like flow'rs of spring un-
lei - se durch den Sinn, Wie Früh - lings - blu - men

fold - ing, It thrill - eth through my soul,
blüht es und schwebt wie Duft da - hin,

118

van - ish quite a - way.
schwin - det wie ein Hauch.

In me - lo - dy ___ deep ___
Und den - noch ruht ___ im ___

hid - den, A fra - grance lies con - cealed, That
Rei - me ver - bor - gen wohl ein Duft, Den

bring - eth tears un - bid - den; Un -
mild aus stil - lem Kei - me ein

dim.

TURN THEN THINE EYES

Henry Purcell

catch - ing, catch - ing flames _____ will on___ thy torch ap -

pear, will on thy torch ap - pear, will on thy torch ap -

pear, ap - pear, will on___ thy torch ap - pear will on___ thy torch ap -

1
2 Fine

pear pear.

ad lib.

WIND OF THE WESTERN SEA

Alfred Tennyson

Graham Peel

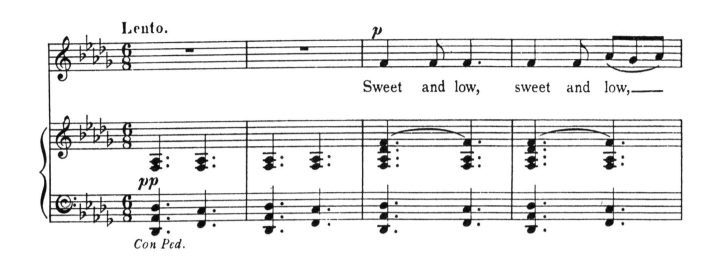

O - ver the roll - ing wa - ters go, Come from the dy - ing

moon, and blow, Blow him a - gain to me, While my lit - tle one,

poco rit.   *p a tempo*

while my pret - ty one sleeps._____   Sleep and rest,

colla voce   *a tempo*

sleep and rest,_____ Fa - ther will come to thee soon;_____

THIS LITTLE ROSE

Emily Dickinson*

William Roy

celerated - - - -

On-ly a bird will won - der,

a tempo

On-ly a breeze will sigh,   Ah, lit-tle rose, how eas - y

For such as thee _____ to die!